Ooey-gooey Animals

Slugs

Lola Schaefer

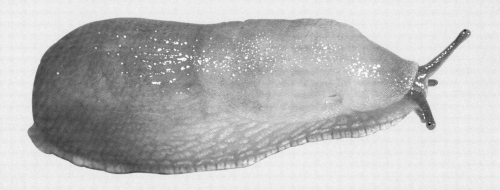

Raintree

www.raintreepublishers.co.uk
Visit our website to find out more information about **Raintree** books.

To order:
☎ Phone 44 (0) 1865 888112
▤ Send a fax to 44 (0) 1865 314091
▢ Visit the Raintree Bookshop at www.raintreepublishers.co.uk to browse our catalogue and order online.

First published in Great Britain by Raintree, Halley Court, Jordan Hill, Oxford OX2 8EJ, part of Harcourt Education.
Raintree is a registered trademark of Harcourt Education Ltd.

Editorial: Nick Hunter and Diyan Leake
Design: Sue Emerson (HL-US) and Joanna Sapwell
Picture Research: Amor Montes de Oca (HL-US)
Production: Lorraine Hicks

Originated by Dot Gradations
Printed and bound in China by South China Printing Company

ISBN 1 844 21025 1
07 06 05 04 03
10 9 8 7 6 5 4 3 2 1

British Library Cataloguing in Publication Data
Schaefer, Lola
Slugs
594.3
A full catalogue record for this book is available from the British Library.

Acknowledgements
The publishers would like to thank the following for permission to reproduce photographs: Color Pic, Inc. p. 21 (E. R. Degginger); Corbis pp. 4 (Frank Lane Picture Agency), 5 (Lawson Wood), 7 (Lawson Wood), 8 (Joe McDonald), 9 (Papilio), 11 (Gallo Images), 15 (Jeffrey L. Rotman), 17 (Jeffrey L. Rotman), 18 (Stephen Frink), 22 (Joe McDonald), 23 (eyestalk and tentacles, Papilio), 24 (Joe McDonald), back cover (eyestalk, Papilio; sea slug, Jeffrey L. Rotman); David Liebman p. 16; Dwight Kuhn pp. 1, 6, 10, 14, 19, 20, 23 (mucus, pest); Jeff Rotman Photography p. 13; National Geographic Society p. 12 (Timothy G. Laman).

Cover photograph of a slug, reproduced with permission of Dwight Kuhn

Every effort has been made to contact copyright holders of any material reproduced in this book. Any omissions will be rectified in subsequent printings if notice is given to the publishers.

CAUTION: Remind children that it is not a good idea to handle wild animals. Children should wash their hands with soap and water after they touch any animal.

Some words are shown in bold, **like this.** You can find them in the glossary on page 23.

Contents

What are slugs?

Slugs are small, soft animals.

They do not have any bones.

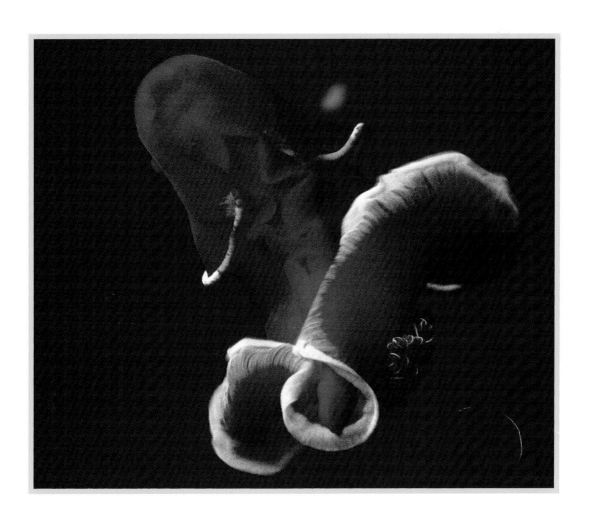

There are lots of different kinds
of slugs.

Where do slugs live?

Some slugs live on land.

They live in damp places like woods and gardens.

Some slugs live in water.

They live in the sea or in small pools on land.

What do slugs look like?

tentacles

Land slugs are yellow, grey or brown.

Sea slugs come in lots of different colours.

eyestalk

eye

Slugs have four **tentacles** on their head.

The two big tentacles are **eyestalks**.

What do slugs feel like?

Land slugs are gooey.

They have **mucus** on their body.

Some sea slugs are smooth.

Some are fluffy.

How big are slugs?

This land slug is smaller than a mushroom.

Some land slugs are as big as a person's hand.

Some sea slugs are small.

Other sea slugs are the size
of an adult's shoe.

How do slugs move?

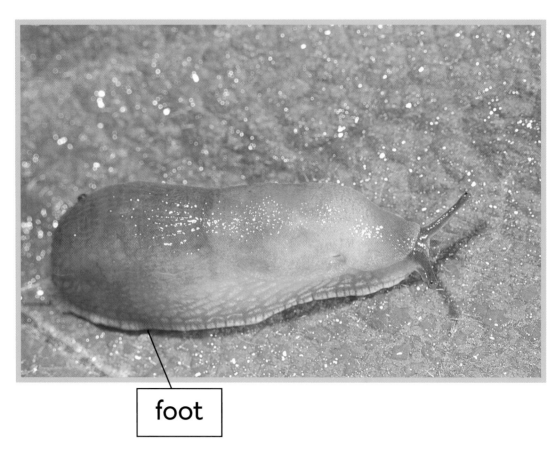

foot

The part that a slug moves along on is its foot.

A land slug wets its foot with **mucus**.

The mucus helps the slug slide along.

Sea slugs swim or crawl in the sea.

What do slugs do all day?

When it is warm, land slugs look for food.

When it gets cold, they dig down into the ground.

Sea slugs are always looking
for food.

What do slugs eat?

sponge

Sea slugs eat other animals in the sea.

Land slugs eat plants and some dead animals.

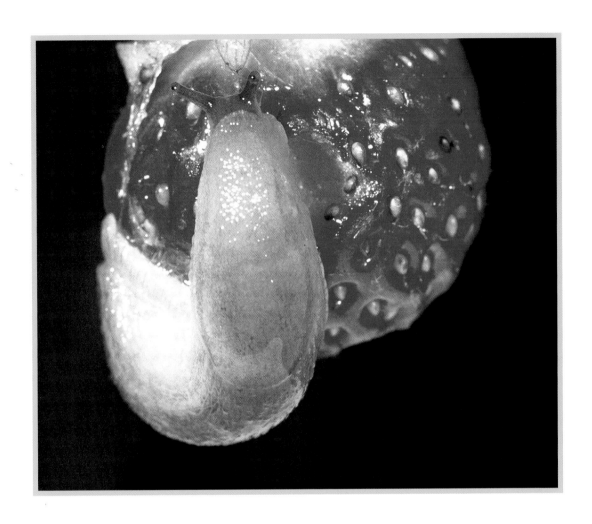

Land slugs can be **pests**.

They eat the things that people plant in their gardens.

Where do new slugs come from?

eggs

Land slugs lay eggs in dark, wet places.

They lay lots of eggs at one time.

These little land slugs are coming out of the eggs.

Quiz

What are these slug parts?

Can you find them in the book?

Look for the answers on page 24.

? ?

Glossary

eyestalk
long part on a slug's head where its eyes are

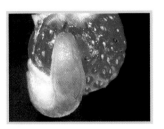

pest
little animal that is bad for people or for people's things

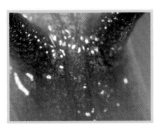

mucus
slimy stuff that some animals have in or on their body

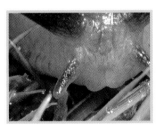

tentacles
long, thin parts that some animals have on their body

Index

Answers to quiz on page 22

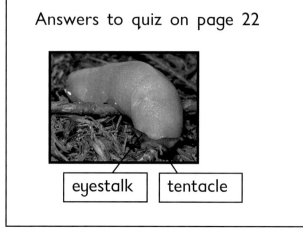

eyestalk   tentacle

Titles in the Ooey-gooey Animals series include:

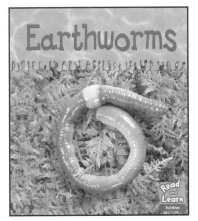

Hardback   1 844 21020 0

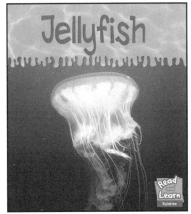

Hardback   1 844 21021 9

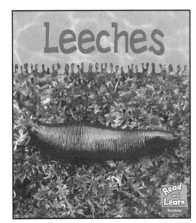

Hardback   1 844 21022 7

Hardback   1 844 21023 5

Hardback   1 844 21024 3

Hardback   1 844 21025 1

Hardback   1 844 21026 X

Find out about the other titles in this series on our website www.raintreepublishers.co.uk